Self-Discipline

The Path to Personal Greatness: Mastering Self-Discipline for a Fulfilling and Purpose-Driven Life

(Elevate Your Life with Self-Discipline: A Comprehensive Guide to Building Strong Habits, Crushing Obstacles, and Attaining Success)

MepeMakris

TABLE OF CONTENT

Improve Your Success. If You Deserve Failure..1

How To Get Over Being Lazy 8

Easy Spy Techniques To Increase Productivity 26

Advanced Timescreening 31

A Comprehensive Guide To Determining Your Objectives 43

Essentials Of Self-Control 50

Reasons To Read This Book 58

The Art Of Manufactured Enticements 62

The Significance Of Focus And Self-Control 71

Morning Routine Customs 76

Self-Control As The Primary Factor In Happiness 82

Self-Control And Sales 91

Cash And Self-Control 92

Develop An Ability To Focus 99

Increasing Control Over Oneself 111

Overcoming Failure With Self-Control 121

Conclusion 125

Improve Your Success. If You Deserve Failure

Visualizing success is a reasonable-sounding idea that you've probably heard before if you've read any self-help books. Imagining success will inspire you to pursue it.

Ironically, as encouraging as that may sound, visualizing achievement really has the opposite effect. It's really more likely to make you fail and make you lazier to visualize victory.

How is that possible?

According to studies, when you visualize achievement, your subconscious is tricked into believing that you have already succeeded. Put differently, it's time to unwind and unwind! You've succeeded! Let's get on that boat, enjoy the sun, margaritas, and sometimes even dunk our feet in the warm, tropical, glistening waters of the Bahamas.

Visualising achievement reduces your chances of success and makes you indolent, according to several research. In a particular study, those who engaged in mental imagery of landing a well-paying job applied for fewer positions and ultimately received a poorer position with a lower salary than those who did not engage in mental imagery (or who used a different visualization technique, as you will discover in the following section). In a similar vein, students who focused on achieving their desired marks ended up studying less and receiving lower grades.

Lesson: Visualising achievement makes you lazy and considerably less likely to succeed in your goals.

What, then is the remedy?

Of course, you may choose to visualize nothing at all, but there's a better, more efficient solution.

Objectives and To-Do List

Setting regular goals is essential to your success, and we'll go into more detail about it in the upcoming chapter. The majority of self-help and achievement literature will emphasize the significance of goal-setting in achieving your aspirations.They should be written twice a day, right after waking up in the morning and right before bed, for optimal results. Although it isn't discussed as often, making a to-do list is unquestionably a hidden gem that is essential to productivity and, eventually, goal achievement. It also doesn't have to take a lot of time; I write my to-do list for the next day at the end of each day in about two minutes.

Advantages

Establish goals is something you undoubtedly hear all the time, but have you ever questioned why? I have, and the reasons are frequently intricate and challenging to comprehend. The same is true for to-do lists. The experts give us complex justifications for making daily to-do lists, yet they nevertheless advise us to do so. These three easy advantages will inspire you to perform both on a daily basis!

Garbage In = Garbage Out states that the mind always generates outcomes that are comparable to what we feed it. And this is precisely what occurs when we write down our objectives and to-do list using a pen and paper. It concentrates not just our conscious mind but also our subconscious mind. Your attention will be fully focused on the objectives you have just considered and put down, as opposed to what was on TV or what your buddies are doing. putting together a strategy in the background, as you sleep to bring your dreams to pass.

Prepare, set, and go!

Making a list of things you want to get done the next day before you go to bed ensures that your day's schedule is set and ready to go when you get up. When the mind is fresh in the morning, it is most creative, therefore, it seems wasteful to use this time for unproductive things like day-planning. Furthermore, since you already know what needs to be done, you will be more productive. You'll know as soon as your eyes open how many things are on your to-do list and how each day will bring you one step closer to realizing your ambitions!

Encourage and awe

You will always face obstacles in life, whether they come from your job, family, health, or religion. Your aspirations and goals will occasionally be the last thing on your mind as a result. Your drive to realize your goals must be strong if you are to persevere through difficult times and never give up. When you've had a difficult week, it's Thursday night, you've just finished the fourth consecutive workday, and it's time to set the alarm for 5.30 am on Friday, you need to be very motivated to get out of bed. This helps to write down your goals both before you go to bed and when you get up. It enables you to stay focused and serves as a reminder of your goals and the reason you began in the first place. It will all be worth it in the end, even the early mornings, late finishes, and sleep-deprived days.

How To Get Over Being Lazy

Sometimes, we feel lazy because we want to avoid doing something, like confront someone or take on a tedious assignment. Other times, we feel lazy because our tasks are so large that we think we need to work as a real team. Sometimes we're just indolent. Either way, it's a quality of our character that we never particularly enjoy. We'll see how to finally beat laziness in this chapter.

Make an effort to identify the true issue. Every time you find yourself getting slack, take a moment to reflect on the situation. Usually, being lazy is a sign of an issue rather than the cause. What is the reason behind your lack of drive? Are you unwell, worn out, afraid, overwhelmed, or are you just trapped and free of stimuli? It's possible that you'll discover that solving the latent issue is simple.

Whatever is preventing you from moving forwards, try your hardest to make it obvious. Usually, it will be one particular element or issue. The only way to address it is, in fact, to identify the reason. You can properly control it once you've identified it.

Concentrate on the actual issue. Now that you are considering the reason behind your indolence, begin by concentrating on it. Although it might not be the instant solution you were hoping for, it will last forever. Remember to take some time to unwind if you're feeling fatigued. Everyone must take a nap. Should your schedule not permit it, you could need to make certain compromises. But there will be an even greater outcome.

Give yourself a break if you're feeling overburdened. How can you make the situation you're in simpler? Can it be divided into smaller, more manageable parts? Can you prioritize things and deal with each one separately?

Ask yourself why you are afraid. It goes without saying that you have some goals in mind. Do you worry that you don't have enough potential? Or do you eventually accomplish your objectives but still need to be satisfied? How can you recognize that your worry is unfounded?

If you're ill, time might be the only solution. Anguish, despair, and other unpleasant feelings are not easily removed. We need time for our wounds to heal. Reducing the urge to end suffering might be the spark that ignites the desired transformation.

What can you alter in your routine if you are unconscious? Is it something mental you need to face, or is it something you can put yourself in a different atmosphere for? How can you breathe new life into each day? Consider using your senses. foods, sounds, locations, music, and so forth.

Develop your organising skills.Even if the congestion is merely visible, it can still seriously impair our ability to be motivated. Do everything within your power to establish order. Clean everything, including your car, desk, home, and habits.

Our subconscious is where a lot of things that we are unaware of occurs. We can tell that there is anything unsettling when we see an unsettling color combination, insufficient light, or an unbalanced area in any other way. Become more organized and get rid of that little but effective deterrent.

Examine your inner monologue.Behaviors can occasionally elicit thoughts, while ideas can occasionally elicit behavior. Confront all possibilities and silence your inner critic. It doesn't help to think things like, "Oh, God, I'm so lazy... Ugh, it's useless!" So give up. That film that is shown internally is entirely under your control.

The question shifts to the positive if you realize you are not performing up to par. "It's been a slow morning, but now it's time to recharge your batteries, and now it's afternoon, I'm working hard!" You'll be shocked at how much the mental optimism wave may truly alter your perspective.

Develop your self-awareness. Too many people never stop to smell the roses. We hastily have a superb dinner in order to reach the dessert, the wine, and our overfull tummies before turning in for the night. Rather than savoring the amazing moment that is now, we are constantly thinking about the next major event. We can make the most of the present moment once we begin to live in it. Bring yourself back to the present the next time you catch yourself daydreaming about the past or the future. Let me show you how wonderful it is to be in the world and to live, whether it's through the scene around you, the food on your fork, or the music playing in your ears. We can sometimes muster the energy to make the most of what we have by pausing and slowing down.

To create a new habit, one must continue the one that has already been formed. This is how self-control is achieved. Go back to the baby. Now, the baby needs to learn how to stand. The infant cannot just sit there; doing so will prevent healthy growth and development. The infant understands that it needs to take one step at a time. The infant performs this before collapsing. There isn't currently a walking circuit in the brain. The infant is going to build one. This implies that the infant will build on one habit to form a new one.

Avoid making the mistake of only seeing the good in others. Believing that everyone is better than you is erroneous. This is a stupid exercise. The only person who matters is the one who is moving forth. Not even identical twins grow at the same speed. Assuming that everyone would advance at the same pace is unfair. This is where it all begins, and it's the way each individual will reach their own objective.

It's time to create a plan once you've acknowledged the beginning point and come to terms with reality. You will be guided towards self-discipline by this plan. Begin with a distinct idea. Establish your objective and choose the first adjustment that has to be made. A life full of failures and sloth cannot be changed quickly. Achieving one objective is necessary before becoming an inspiration to others. Establishing the objective and creating a strategy to get it are both necessary. Writing it down and referring to it several times a day is a smart idea. Written objectives are more specific than vague aspirations.

Please get rid of any temptation that can make it more difficult for you to accomplish your objective. If you want to lose weight, get rid of any bad meals. You can throw away the smoke if your ultimate Goal is to stop smoking. There may be instances when you need to make changes to specific areas of your daily routine. If your daily commute passes the best doughnut store and you're trying to lose weight, you might need to find a different route to work.

Make your objective simple. Achievable goals tend to be simpler than more complex ones. The objective "to quit smoking" may seem too difficult for someone who has smoked for a long time and is still highly dependent on smoking. It is advisable to start with a modest goal. To begin with, smoke outside only—never inside the house. No smoking is allowed inside the home, not even during blizzards or storms. There are times when going outside to smoke just isn't worth it. You've just accomplished your first objective. It's no longer smoke in the house. Then, give up smoking in your vehicle. Smoking is a habit that is both mental and physical. It's critical to conquer cravings and establish a new neural pathway in order to stop smoking. Positive objectives include getting rid of any residual smoke odor from clothing and leaving the house and car smelling better. If you clean the kitchen counter or go for a walk down the street, you might be able to delay the temptation to smoke. This is how negative habits can be swapped out for positive ones, while positive habits promote self-control.

It is important to value willpower. It is common knowledge that a stubborn individual is one who is resistant to change. The obstinate individual has will. Stubbornness is a fancy word for willpower. Act unyielding. Establish your goals in advance, and don't allow anything to get in the way of them. Aim for your objective. Never take "no" for an answer. Keep your aim constant no matter what. Reaching your objectives requires sturdiness.

Start by making a plan. Next, draft a backup plan. Any plan that has a fallback in place is better than none at all. A significant element of weight loss will be adopting healthy eating habits. At home, where you have total control over the menu, this is simple to accomplish. When you get the invitation to the party, what happens? Connecting with friends and family over a well-planned party is a terrific idea. And the food, all of it? This is the backup plan. You have a fallback strategy in place to eat less already. Maybe the idea is to sample everything with one mouthful and then mingle with other guests for the remainder of the evening. The second plan is this one. This will guarantee that the aim is maintained and aid to maintain the original plan in place.

When the aim is accomplished, remember to reward them with a treat. Rewarding excellent behavior is what makes people happy. Select a reward that fits the objective. You can give up smoking in your home and paint the walls. Your home will smell wonderful and look fantastic. If the vehicle has not been smoked in, it is worthwhile to get it detailed. A brand-new automobile has an amazing scent. If your weight loss goals have been met, treat yourself to a new wardrobe.

Recognize that mistakes will happen occasionally. It doesn't imply that you ought to aim for failure. This entails accepting failure as it occurs. People are people. It will not work.

Though they will occasionally fail, they will attempt. Acknowledge that failure is unavoidable. Recognise your failure. Avoid feeling resentful or guilty. These feelings are common and might get in the way of your goal-achieving efforts. Take lessons from your errors. How did it turn out? What took place? What steps may be taken to ensure that this does not occur again? Failure can be overcome if it has been recognized and examined. You are still headed in the correct direction. It might require some adjusting. There may have to be a small bend. Regaining your focus is the first step towards accomplishing any goal. Additionally, this is the beginning of self-discipline.

There is a significant growth in self-sufficiency. Individuals who have proven to be capable of setting and achieving objectives are far more adept at looking after themselves. Based on the objectives they have already met and those they hope to accomplish in the future, they develop a vision of what it means to live. They are also far more adept at setting and carrying out plans to achieve future objectives. These individuals are well aware of their full potential.

Furthermore, improved self-control improves interpersonal connections. Self-control advocates perceive their clients as more dependable and trustworthy. People are far better at meaning and keeping promises made to others when they learn to work towards goals and learn to keep those promises with themselves.

Being disciplined can save a lot of time. Self-disciplined people are in charge of their everyday actions. Those who are disciplined don't put things off and do tasks when they should. People will save a great deal of time and energy only from this. The days of stressing over what will and won't get done at the last minute are over. This makes living a more composed and tranquil life possible.

Now that you're well on your way to living a disciplined and self-controlled life, it's time to unwind a little before tackling the next objective.

Some pointers for self-honesty:

Recall that there is no harm in putting things in writing. You can decide to keep it private, update it, destroy it, or share it with no one.
. If you need help figuring out where to start, consider doing a personality test. They can give you some insight into your nature to help you get started, but they need help finding you. A test may help you begin to know and be true to yourself.
. Seek outside assistance if you are still determining your desires. Ask your friends, consult a counselor, and take a test.
. Regardless of the progress you are making, you can always seek professional assistance. You don't have to work alone to be honest with yourself.

Step 5: Discover Your Drive

Motivation is necessary for self-control and devotion. In actuality, motivation and self-discipline are positively correlated. Self-discipline qualities increase with your level of motivation and focus. Your encouragement and drive to work harder will increase as you concentrate more on developing self-discipline.

Finding motivation might be challenging at times. It may run away from us and seem completely useless. Even the most disciplined and driven individuals occasionally struggle with motivation. In fact, there are moments when we are in such a rut that it seems impossible even to consider changing for the better.

Inspiration is still there. You can begin your journey towards good change by taking a few modest actions. It can occasionally feel unattainable. Recall that you are not by yourself. These are some useful resources to concentrate on motivation. You may keep going and increase your motivation by doing the following:

One objective. Once you've completed your One Goal, you may always work on your other objectives. Select one and proceed accordingly. You can perform the following task and so on if you can perform the first one.

Look for motivation. Consult the web, your loved ones, your pals, animals, and literature. Look for anything that motivates you. Look for anything to encourage you.

Get giddy.

Create a sense of anticipation. This advice may seem difficult, and many individuals will ignore it. However, it does work. Wait to jump into a goal, even if it inspires you. Choose a future day, such as a week, two, or even a month, and designate that as your Start day. Could you put it in your calendar?

This is a fantastic method to feel optimistic about the future. Revel in the upcoming date. Make this the most significant date of your life. Draught a strategy of action. You are creating anticipation and concentrating more of your energy and attention on your Goal by starting later than usual.

Set a goal post. Print out your objective in bold font. Please put it in a place where you will see it frequently. Remind yourself and keep it posted. Maintain an optimistic attitude and strong drive.

Admit in public. Inform your loved ones of your actions. Inform people about your actions. If you can find support for yourself, your motivation will increase.

Seek assistance. It's challenging to complete a task by yourself. Locate your support system, whether it be online, offline, or both. This will assist and motivate you more. Strong motivators include family, friends, and support. They'll be happy with you. This sense of pride inspires and supports you more. When you finish, you will have even more to look forward to.

Continue as is. Never give up, no matter what you do. Don't give up even if you're lacking motivation today or this week. That drive will return once more. When you find out, know that it will return stronger than before.

Expand upon minor achievements.

Each day, read about it. Employ weblogs. Consult books and the internet for advice. Read about others who are making use of and abusing their abilities. Study other people's self-control. Check out what other people are writing about. Take a look at what the other Read about the wonderful experiences of those who achieve the same achievement that you aspire to achieve in the future.

Ask for assistance when your motivation wanes. Having issues? Seek assistance. Give your loved ones a call. Search online.

Consider the advantages rather than the challenges. Consider and concentrate on the positive outcomes that will follow from achieving your objectives. This is incredibly inspiring.

Negative thoughts should be squashed and replaced with optimistic ones. Goodness grows from positivity. Refrain from letting your mind dwell on bad things. Allow them to assist you. For both you and those around you, maintaining a positive outlook may have a profound impact.

Easy Spy Techniques To Increase Productivity

It's no secret that CIA personnel undergo demanding training to increase their productivity. Here are some tips you can use to increase your productivity.

Direct Attention

Taking care of work that needs to be done right away is the first and most important tip. Let's take an example where you receive an email that requires a prompt response. Don't waste any more time in doing this. Things is a mistake to put things off because doing so will make them seem less important and encourage sloth. It is better to only do it if you have finished it by the deadline. This will inspire you to complete your assignments on time every time.

First, tough

As I have said before, you must start with the more difficult chores and work your way down to the easier ones when you go about your daily duties. At first, this may seem a little overwhelming, but as you become used to putting the most challenging and crucial tasks first, it will quickly come naturally to you.

As usual, start by listing all of the things you need to do in a given day and then group them according to difficulty. When you have the most physical and mental energy, tackle the difficult or complex tasks first. This will ensure that you have enough time to complete the simpler tasks that require less effort to clean up.

Haste

In order to complete every assignment you take on properly and on time, instill a sense of urgency in yourself. I was hoping you could make a list, rank your chores according to priority and difficulty, and start with the items at the top of the list, as I mentioned earlier. One useful tip is to set a lower time limit for each task so that you may complete it more quickly without rushing. A number of times for every activity, and then carry them out appropriately.

Get up early

Rising early is among the most crucial tips to follow if you want to increase your productivity. It will be essential that you grow by five or six in order to have ample time to work out, organize your schedule, and prepare a nutritious breakfast for yourself. People who rise late are inevitably more anxious and have a less pleasant day's conclusion. This can be easily avoided by just arranging your day and increasing an hour earlier than usual. It would be best if you went to bed at least an hour earlier than normal because you will need to sleep sooner in order to wake up earlier. Avoid engaging in diversions right before bed, as they might significantly disrupt this pattern.

Motivation

To increase productivity, inspiration is crucial when it comes to completing work. In the book's introduction, I touched on the significance of this. This could be your objectives or a role model. Take 30 minutes each day to think about these and find inspiration every day. Some people find that reading positive affirmations and motivational phrases helps them stay energized. You, too, may increase your productivity by doing the same.

Advanced Timescreening

You have to become an expert time manager if you want total control over your life. You should carefully study this article to grasp the importance of time management because time is a vital resource.

If you're someone who doesn't value your time, why is time management so important? Are you aware that if you want to succeed in the future, this is the most crucial skill to acquire and become proficient in?

If you don't manage your time well, coincidences will take over your life. You will ultimately end up doing what other people want you to do, and you will never be in control of your life.

You'll start to take charge of your life by learning time management skills and managing your studies. It will be up to you to take the initiative and make the decision on where you want to go.

You will surely reap several benefits when you manage your time well. Once you have mastered it properly, you will be able to work more, play more, and learn faster than before.

The Value of Time Management in Your Life

- You Acquire More Fruitful Hours

If you are good with time management, you will profit from more productive hours. Instead of wasting time idly browsing the internet or chatting with your coworkers, you will be more disciplined at work.

Think about extending your day by one useful hour. This is equivalent to an extra five hours each week or about 250 hours annually. This is equivalent to an additional six weeks of work in a year.

- You Increase Efficiency and Productivity

If you are good at time management, you will be able to accomplish more in less time. Gaining experience from completing more assignments can help you immensely in achieving your objectives.

Your ability to focus better will enable you to give everything you do much more attention. You will grow more quickly than others who need to practice time management skills.

You'll enjoy more pleasure and free time.

You need to develop good time management skills if you want to enjoy your life. This will enable you to experience all you desire, live life to the fullest, and do the things you want to do.

You will work fewer hours and achieve more since your working hours will become more productive. You'll have extra free time as a consequence to spend with your family. You will also learn the value of restful sleep, which will provide you with more energy and happiness as you finish your task.

You'll Be in Charge of Your

The last benefit of time management is that it will provide you with total control over the trajectory of your life. To put it simply, you are ultimately in control of your life. Your comprehension of the tasks at hand and the work that needs to be done will improve.

You'll learn to be more organized, which will help you avoid running behind schedule. You won't ever have a deadline emergency, and while others are still stressed out over their work, you'll be spending more time relaxing.

Never worry that you'll get tense or rigid with time; rather, the opposite will happen. Because you won't be as dependent on outside events to manage your time, you'll have more freedom. You will take control of your time instead of someone else by practicing time management.

I'm going to walk you through how to saddle up your free time and ride that baby all the way to your goals in the next four steps!

1. Making a schedule (well, making a list in writing)

The most crucial step in regaining control over your leisure time is to make a detailed inventory of your resources and allocate them appropriately by putting them on paper. Although it may seem apparent, I can't tell you how many people I know who have their calendars in their minds and still expect to finish everything. People tend to forget things, so I hate to break the news to those of you who believe that by doing this, you can maximize your productivity. Still, the truth is that eventually, you will also forget something that you would have remembered if you had written it down.

And no, you don't always need to carry a notebook and pencil because—you know—you have a smartphone. That would be the one you have with you at the moment, or perhaps the one you're using to read this book. That device isn't just an effective means of maintaining relationships with the people and things you need to stay in touch with; it's also your very own personal helper, helping you make the most of your leisure time so you can start moving toward your goals.

Just open a blank document or list software (I like Evernote) every Sunday night, or before the day you want your week to begin, and name it "To-Do This Week." That's all it takes. Then, just put your goals for the coming week in writing.

Work out
Begin arranging your travel.
Sort through the flat and list a few items on Craigslist, etc.

2. Dissect it

After you've made your list, you need to calculate how much free time you have in total and divide it up so that your to-do list can fit in. You can organize things as you choose, but I find that breaking things up into the days of the week helps.

For instance:

Three hours of exercise (Monday, Wednesday, and Friday from 7 to 8 a.m. to 8 p.m.)
Begin arranging your travel: Two hours (7 pm–8 pm on Monday and 7 pm–8 pm on Thursday)
Clear clutter and make online sales: Two hours (7 p.m. on Tuesday and 8 p.m. on Thursday).

This way, you'll be able to know exactly when and how long you need to start doing something. This is quite beneficial for achieving both short- and long-term objectives since it helps you divide the work into smaller, more manageable portions so that you are not overwhelmed by it all at once.

In addition to the conventional physical workouts, you can work on your self-discipline and willpower by practicing the following activities.

You're seated on a train or bus. Then an elderly man or woman, or a pregnant woman, enters. You take a seat for them after getting up. Yes, you do the right thing, but you also do this because you enjoyed staying seated in the first place. You learn how to perform anything you are hesitant to undertake through this practise. You can conquer your body's, mind's, and emotions' resistance with the aid of this workout.

The washbasin is filled with multiple filthy dishes. You're thinking that I might clean them tomorrow or later. Now get up and tidy them. Don't let your laziness to rule you; overcome it. By taking this action, you are strengthening yourself. It will become simpler for you to act right away as a result of your victory over laziness and the urge to put things off.

After a tiring day at work, you instantly sit down on the couch and begin watching TV. Even if you should take a shower first, you need to be in the mood. Resist the want to curl up in front of the TV; instead, get up and take a shower.

You enjoy having sugar with your brew. Thus, give up adding sugar to your coffee for a week.

You read the newspaper's gossip section just like everyone else. Give up reading rumours for a week.

You have always used the lift. Even if it's just for a few days, you've now decided to take the stairs.

Brains & Ideas

Achieving self-discipline also requires maintaining good mental and spiritual health, much like with food, exercise, and sleep. You must regularly engage in mindfulness meditation. The advantages of mindfulness are as follows:

elevates your emotional intelligence and mood

fosters the growth of healthy social relationships

aids in preventing emotional drinking, smoking, and eating

increases resistance to suffering and misfortune

increases self-acceptance and self-esteem

reduces anxiety, concern, and impulsive behavior. Reduces fear, stress, despair, and loneliness

improves concentration and mental fortitude

improved mental abilities and original thought

Improved judgement and problem-solving skills

Boosts energy and the immune system

enhances bodily well-being and guards against numerous diseases

This is a daily mindfulness activity that you can do.

The simplest yet most powerful type of mindfulness meditation is mindful breathing. The activity

Establish a comfortable, upright sitting position: Keep your back away from the back of the chair while you sit comfortably. Steady your spine, if you can. Ascertain that the temperature in the room is comfortable for you and that you won't be bothered by anyone or anything for the next ten or so minutes. If you're comfortable with it, close your eyes.

Try your hardest to concentrate on your breathing. Remind yourself that you don't have to be critical or judgmental of yourself if your thoughts stray to other ideas and emotions. Give up on any notion of what might occur in the future. Allow whatever transpires to occur.

Keep your breathing in mind: Shut the eyes. With every breath, notice how it enters and exits your nose, how it expands and contracts your chest and abdomen, and how it passes through the back of your throat. Try to feel the breath coming in and going out while you place your hands on your abdomen. Keep your focus on the tummy when you place your hands there. Allow your breathing to occur at its natural depth and pace. It doesn't matter if your breathing steadily increases in depth or decreases over time; either technique is acceptable. Accept the way your breathing is now.

Refocus your attention gently back to your breathing. Even when you do this, your thoughts and feelings may stray into other realms, including fancies, dreams, and ideas. This is what our minds typically do, and it's perfectly natural. When this occurs, acknowledge where your thoughts have wandered and gently bring them back to your breathing, much like when you turn a car. Recall that an essential component of any mindfulness practice is getting your distracted attention back to the present moment. If you find yourself becoming irritated or disappointed with yourself, smile softly, take a deep breath, and return your attention to your breathing.

After practicing for ten minutes, slowly open your eyes and take note of your feelings.

A Comprehensive Guide To Determining Your Objectives

Step 1: Write down all of the things you need to get done in the morning.

Finish each task as it comes up. Avoid getting too attached to any one task. Permit the momentum and gratification that arise from finishing a task to transfer to the subsequent one.

Step 2: See your final destination.

Think about your actual life goals. Here, I'm talking about your long-term goals.

Think about your response if you found yourself in that circumstance. Think about how you would appear if you lead such a life. Prior to and following the completion of a daily task, think back to this vision.

By doing this, you create something bigger out of all the little, detailed things you're doing now. This serves as a reminder to your conscious and subconscious minds that everything you do right now matters. You will eventually achieve the great triumph you have been striving for with each step you take right now.

Step 3: Every day, jot down your lofty goals for yourself.

Your grand vision should be put in writing as soon as you wake up. Once you have read and visualized the paper, crumple it. Then rewrite it, beginning with a blank piece of paper.

When you do this, you are invigorating both your conscious and subconscious minds. You also get rid of less significant visions and objectives. Perhaps you believe that because they are desired by others, you must pursue them.

But when you renew your life's big picture in this way, a lot of the unnecessary stuff gets cut out. The things that really matter in life are what are left. These are the goals for the long run. These are the things that you know in your heart of hearts will always be significant to you.

Step 4: Consciously recommit to your long-term objective.

Despite the possibility of coming across as cliche, you need to look at your list of aspirational goals and tell yourself, "I am capable." I've decided to keep this for myself. "I'm going to do it."

I'm giving you a few places to start. Go ahead and make your version. Here, it's crucial that you consciously choose to follow through on these.

Please remember that it will take time to accomplish these goals. It does indeed require a great deal of sacrifice.

The good news is that you will commit these to memory by trying to be as conscious of them as you can. Writing down your goals, rewriting them, and folding them up makes it a daily ritual. It eventually absorbs into your being.

Step 5: Take action to achieve your goals.

Consider how your daily tasks align with your goals as you complete them. Tell yourself some encouraging things about your accomplishments and how they moved you one step closer to your objective at the end of the day.

Because of this, you will be able to overcome procrastination. This encourages you to give it everything you've got in order to accomplish your goals.

Additionally, by taking this step, you can be sure that your goals are top of mind. They are not some far-off dream or optimistic notion that would be nice to come true. Rather, it happens instantly.

Detailed instructions for developing a self-sustaining incentive system

Step 1: Consider your life's accomplishments

Everyone has accomplished something. Consider those accomplishments. How do they describe you? Which strengths are you able to name? What character attributes are you able to strengthen? Get giddy over those.

Step 2: Determine what your primary competencies and strengths are perceived by others.

For what reasons do people admire you? When they examine your life and your life's work, who do they see? Make no error. We can all take pride in something. Think about those.

Step #3: Acknowledge that the things you have accomplished are the results of processes.

Your accomplishments weren't given to you. Let's be clear about that. They required labour from you. They participate in a procedure. You still had to work for it, no matter how long it was.

Determine the nature of those procedures. Recognize that the processes you are going through now are similar to the ones you went through previously.

Step 4: Make a connection between the current process and the ones you've previously gone through.

You should feel a great sense of relief when you recognize that the process you are going through on your path to greater success is actually not all that different from a similar path you have previously taken.

It's not like you're doing something entirely new. You've already traveled this route. You should feel at ease knowing this. You're not venturing into unknown territory. Best feature? It is nothing new for you. Why are you not doing it right now?

You've done this process before, so get excited about it. It has already produced fruitful outcomes. Hold off until this journey produces even better outcomes. This is how you start to get excited about the process rather than just being fixated on the result.

Essentials Of Self-Control

Every year, we have the opportunity to make a fresh start, set new objectives, achieve recent successes, and let go of negative habits, ideas, and problems that are preventing us from moving forward. The secret to success in all spheres—health, fitness, and business—is self-discipline. It is entirely our responsibility; you must learn how to do it by being consistent and determined to finish even when you don't feel like it.

Our lack of self-discipline, inability to postpone gratification, failure to see how decisions we make today will affect our future tomorrow, inability to say no to new responsibilities or obligations, and careless use of time, money, and energy are the root causes of our many frustrations, sadness, and disharmony in our relationships and on a personal level. It takes time to develop; it begins with tiny, daily habits, such as putting off a business call you have to make today or starting a book you've been meaning to read but keep putting off.

Over time, this causes you to develop crippling self-insecurity; you stop feeling like the person who always sticks to their word and must follow through. Simple things like keeping your home neat and orderly, your workspace clear, and your clothes hung up rather than strewn all over your room are signs of self-discipline. I'm not saying you have to be obsessive or compulsive; it's just about having that inner glow that comes from being able to handle small tasks well before moving on to larger, more important projects. As you begin to practice the art of self-discipline, it becomes more ingrained in every aspect of your life. People are searching for spiritual magic pills that will provide them with relief from their problems without requiring them to make any sacrifices. We want to enjoy life to the fullest and don't want to suffer the consequences. Making self-discipline your main priority will help you notice that your energy is more internally focused and isn't being sapped by chaos or issues in your life. Your point is retained and channeled towards activities you enjoy, such as writing, hiking, exercising, or just spending time in nature. The human mind is wired for instant gratification, and overcoming this tendency requires a great deal of self-control.

An additional frequent barrier to achieving the aim is stress. If a person is experiencing great stress, they may decide to choose self-indulgence over the difficult path that leads to their goal. People who are under pressure often eat badly or not at all, avoid physical activity, and smoke excessively. When under stress, people can lose their temper and stop taking care of their loved ones or their homes for no apparent reason. They frequently need to remember to follow through on their promises, particularly when they are made with the intention of achieving particular objectives.

Self-control is impacted by stress. If self-control is absent, self-discipline will not flourish. It is not uncommon to forget well-intentioned behaviors and fall back into harmful ones while under pressure. When this occurs, self-control starts to decline. By accepting the chance that it might occur and making a backup plan, this can be easily avoided. Have a backup plan ready to prevent succumbing to stress, just as one was developed to resist temptation during the celebration. Create a backup plan to include relaxation techniques in everyday activities. The activities are infinite and include reading, taking a hot bath, walking, meditating, and listening to music. What matters is that this is perceived as a pleasurable pastime and is employed as a stress-relieving strategy to prevent a spike in tension.

In most cases, clearing out the garage is a bad idea while trying to reduce stress. Certain activities will cause tension on their own. Seek out the soothing pursuits.

Long-term work is necessary to achieve self-discipline as a long-term objective. One of the most frequent issues people run into when trying to form disciplined habits is underestimating the amount of work required to reach each objective. People demand immediate outcomes. Too far off is someday. Individuals frequently attempt complete life makeovers at once. They will establish multiple goals at once and assume that they will all be easily attained and last indefinitely. In actuality, even highly self-disciplined individuals must work towards new objectives gradually. It's a good idea to occasionally schedule brief, structured breaks. A goal to reduce weight is a good thing. But if regular meals, or even days, are built in for a little cheating, it will be easier to achieve and look less like a punishment. We are all human. The strongest people can withstand temptation for eternity. Like the party plan, incorporating a meal to cheat on a diet plan makes it less of an attraction and more of a backup plan to get past a setback. Knowing there will be a treat at the end of the week will make it easier to follow the diet plan.

There are more ways to include backup plans that permit some "cheating" in order to prevent being caught off guard by significant obstacles. Put in a lot of effort at work, but schedule regular downtime to unwind and refuel. Work out hard and frequently, but give your body time to heal by taking days off. Work hard in your studies, but make time for the occasional night out or TV-watching session. Since humans are not robots, they can only run continuously with either tiring out or breaking down. Without regular pauses, the objective quickly turns into something to be hated.

Work out

Everyone is aware of the advantages of exercise. Still, very few people exercise on a daily basis. People's perception of practice as a laborious task is the main cause of this. They never get to the stage where working out becomes a regular because they keep coming up with reasons not to start. But it would be best if you took up exercise. Exercise is associated with better willpower and mental function. Exercise also enhances blood flow. Naturally, oxygen is carried by blood, which improves focus and mental clarity.

Additionally, exercising makes you feel amazing about yourself, which strengthens your resolve to make wise decisions. The secret to exercising is to figure out what kind of physical exercise suits you best. For instance, some people can dance for hours on end yet detest running. Love for physical exercise will make you eager to engage in it, which will strengthen your resolve and help you grow as a person.

Get enough rest.

Sleep is essential for the body to repair itself. This explains why it's risky to sleep too little. It causes severe damage to the prefrontal cortex. This region aids in managing your stress reaction and desires. Getting enough sleep provides your brain with the energy it needs to function properly. You cannot use willpower if you do not know why you make the decisions that you do. You'll be less susceptible to outside influences when you have faith in your beliefs. Getting enough sleep also helps you think clearly when you approach issues and look for workable answers. Don't undervalue sleep as a result. Just like with any other significant endeavor, prepare for it. Establish a sleep schedule that will allow you to enjoy your slumber and decide when you want to go to bed. Make sure you get six hours of sleep or more.

Reasons To Read This Book

If you've downloaded this book, you've undoubtedly come to the realization that changing your life by wishing and hoping won't be enough. You've also concluded that forcing yourself to adopt a new lifestyle or shift has yet to succeed. You may have made multiple attempts to "just do it," only to discover that your previously formed sense of purpose is overwhelmed by your ingrained behaviors or habits.

It isn't very comforting to realize this, yet there is positive news to report. You've made a significant initial move by taking ownership of your actions. We will discuss responsibility frequently in this book since it is a key idea. Essentially, the hard reality is that you must base your self-discipline on self-responsibility if you want your life to change. You must come to terms with the fact that no one else is capable of managing your life for you, beginning at this very moment. You are the only one who can make the necessary modifications. It's your fault.

How to Benefit from This Book

This book will only take you around thirty minutes to read, yet it contains many important lessons that have the power to alter your life. You'll discover:

- How to set flexible, life-changing goals; - How to identify your weaknesses and support your new ways of thinking and living when things go wrong; - The mental strategies you need to be a truly self-disciplined person; - The character traits that form the basis for self-discipline; - How to deal with the reactions of others when you start to change.

Pose This Question to Yourself

You would be correct if, after reading this introduction, you feel that practicing self-discipline is going to take a lot of effort. At the first obstacle, it can be easy to give up on any chance of improving oneself. There is a lot of work ahead of you, and it will require all of your patience, commitment, and time. Thus, why should you bother?

Now, here's the situation. Imagine the upcoming year, or the following five, or the next ten. That period will pass whether or not you take action. At some time, barring your demise, you will have to confront the repercussions of your choices—or, in certain situations, the implications of your inaction. What you need to do is ask yourself: How do you want to feel when that time comes? Assume at the moment that you are reading this book that you are 21 years old. Imagine yourself at the age of 31 in ten years. Imagine that you attempted to achieve your goals with either no action or very little action. Knowing that you have squandered years of potential, how would the older version of yourself feel? Perhaps you won't mind at all. Maybe you'll sidestep the matter entirely or adopt a philosophical stance.

Why, though, bet? Why take the chance of experiencing depression and discouragement due to your inability to take advantage of the possibilities that are presented to you? Isn't it preferable to take advantage of every opportunity that presents itself and work hard to develop a lifetime of dependable mental habits? Flip to the next page and get going.

The Art Of Manufactured Enticements

Sonja Lyubomirsky, the author of "The How of Happiness," claims that only 10% of human happiness is influenced by external influences, 40% by internal causes, and 50% by heredity. These outside variables include things like your marital status and possession of an iPhone, among other things. This means that possibly much less than you realized, only 10% of your happiness is dependent on outside circumstances.

Even so, how many people pursue inner science? Our pursuit of happiness through the gratification of one or more materialistic desires at a time never stops. Every time our financial and superficial enjoyment fades away, we are left feeling empty inside. When our senses—the eye to see, the ear to hear, the nose to smell, the tongue to taste, the body to tangibles, and the mind to thoughts—come into touch with sense objects, this barrier is triggered.

Buddhist teaching discourses describe desire as follows: "Imagine a bowl of water mixed with lac, turmeric, or red dye. When you add turmeric to the water, watch how it spreads throughout the entire surface and gives the water its unique colour." Similar to this, temptations expand to new heights when they are ignored, seizing the mind's capacity to become an addiction. Our attachment to our desires is the source of our anxiety and melancholy.

Is there any desire that does not originate from our senses or is not materialistic? The quest for enlightenment and the ultimate truth originate in our minds and senses, don't they? So what exactly is meant by a "hindrance to mind"? Isn't the goal of enlightenment itself to know the ultimate truth or to live a pain-free life?

Understanding this conclusion is difficult, and numerous hypotheses exist that center around it. Some advise choosing between one's right and incorrect desires. I found it to be completely ineffective. Our outdated mentality can deceive us into thinking that our desires are the finest options for us at that particular moment. Haven't you heard? I'm under stress! I must have a drink or a smoke!

The alternative idea holds that the right wants are those that liberate. Once more, it didn't help when I needed a smoke, a drink, or to indulge in some emotional shopping. The idea that I would be enslaved if I didn't do this deceived me into believing that it was what was liberating.

Certain irresistible desires, like smoking and drug abuse, are obvious, but others, like compulsive eating and emotional shopping, go unrecognized in our society. This could be because eating, shopping, or simply scrolling through your Facebook, Instagram, and TicToc feeds on a daily basis are less socially stigmatized.

There are a lot of contradictory events and things going on in the world right now, and looking at everything from the perspective of a pessimist can make life even more depressing and disappointing. You definitely don't need that to happen.

These are two suggestions that you might find helpful if you are trying to eliminate negative ideas from your mind and you are looking for classes on how to overcome counterintuitive thinking.

Take control of your emotions. A surge of emotion frequently puts you in a situation where you lose self-control and end up doing bad things that you will probably regret later. There are undoubtedly many challenges and unpleasant surprises in life, and once you go through one, you'll undoubtedly lose control of your emotions and unintentionally make a happy mistake of making judgements that aren't entirely positive. If you can manage your emotions, you can also assist yourself in overcoming these problems in daily life and developing into a better, more positive person.

Find ways to make a difference in the lives of others every day, even in small ways. Making time to assist others is another strategy that can assist you in overcoming the effects of contradictory reasoning. Giving and helping others is a great way to encourage the development of positive habits in yourself and, of course, it will also boost your positive energy. Contributing to and assisting others will also help you realize how minor your problems are in comparison to those of others.

Remember to use more positive language than those that are negative. Unbeknownst to you, but there are a tonne of crucially bad words spoken every day that might negatively affect your attitude as well. The more you complain about how miserable your life is, how unfortunate you are, etc., the more likely it is that these things will happen.

Learn how to pay attention to upbeat songs and stories, and learn how to stay a strategic distance away from tattle no matter what. Your attitude is greatly influenced by what you hear, see, and look around you. The more unpleasant and depressing music and gossip you constantly listen to, the more of an impact they will have on you.

Establish the norm of not whimpering or complaining. You may not be able to stop complaining or crying in this life, especially if things don't go your way. However, if you keep complaining and whining, you may also acquire this bad habit, which will make you become a hostile person who always finds the bad in everything.

Go with positive individuals. Being surrounded by and connected to helpful people is, in fact, one of the easiest ways to be a productive person. An optimistic outlook and an upbeat mindset are contagious. Try to identify the kind of individuals you are hanging out with because if you accept positive people, you will also be one of them.

Just six items can be kept in mind when determining whether or not to overcome counterintuitive reasoning. Similarly, keep in mind that you may definitely overcome negative thought patterns and enjoy a happier existence.

Tips for a Positive Attitude: 5 Easy Steps to Get Rid of Negative Thoughts

These suggestions for adopting a good attitude will make a big difference in your life and assist you in overcoming the negative thinking that drags you down in day-to-day living. The amusing thing about people in the public glare is how unhappy they are with their lives. That is, generally speaking, because they need help to recognize what is realistic for them since opposing arguments overpower them. Their lives would be filled with happiness and success if they could take noteworthy steps to overcome erroneous beliefs.

If you are someone who is always trying to overcome contrary reasoning, then make the time to learn the key positive demeanor strategies in this article. Once you do, and you put them into practice, you will soon notice a positive change in your life and understand exactly how to overcome contrary reasoning.

The Significance Of Focus And Self-Control

Focus and self-discipline are crucial since they serve as the cornerstone for achieving remarkable outcomes and performance.

If you are unable to concentrate, you are, by definition, dispersed (also known as fragmented, as people frequently say). And the outcome of this is that nothing stays the same; you start with one thing, move on to the next, go back, and then move on to something else. all to no purpose. You might try to do something that you truly need to do. And no matter how hard you try, nothing works. Eventually, items on your to-do list begin to resurface and haunt you day after day, week after week, much like a monster from a bad movie.

You will suffer, quite literally, for the rest of your life if you lack self-direction. You won't be able to act and take action when necessary to improve your future. This is due to the fact that It is the process by which we link disparate systems and ideas together to create coherence. It is the life force that drives everything else.

How to enhance focus with direction "How can I enhance my focus?" Many people find this issue upsetting since they frequently find themselves in situations where these abilities are needed, yet they realize that they lack them. You must develop these skills in order to apply them.

These abilities are not taught in school, and the majority of people need to be made aware of how to develop them. In addition to this, we come across several situations and diëtractions every day that prevent us from focusing, weakening our direction and resolutions.

People will agree that self-discipline and focus are important and required skills if you ask them about them. They do, however, think that they are difficult to acquire abilities. They believe that enhancing them would necessitate a significant amount of time and effort, which they would rather invest.

Honing your focus and discipline indeed takes time and effort on your part, but it's easy. Every day, people spend hours watching TV, engaging in gossip, sending texts, and using their mobile phones. But in order to enhance self-distance and concentration, you require only a fraction of this time.

"An undisciplined mind leads to suffering, and a disciplined mind leads to happiness."

- Dalai Lama

For other people, maintaining a regimen is a chore. It's a type of order that frees me up to soar, for me."

- Andrews, Julie

"When faced with challenging circumstances, if you focus on the possible, you can positively alter your appearance, lessen your stress, and focus on achieving goals that might not have been possible for someone else."

- Catherine Piercer

The challenging aspect of enhancing discourse and outline is remembering to continuously improve them, even when it seems like they are coming to an end. Additionally, since your mind dislikes change and discipline, it may put up some resistance. It is important to ignore your mind.

One strategy for persevering and never giving up is to constantly remind yourself of the reasons you require these skills and how they will benefit you in your life.

Maintaining focus and discipline increases your ability to follow through on everything you undertake. This is a very helpful skill that will help you follow through with your goals and ambitions and achieve your promises and resolutions. The more focus and discipline you put in, the easier it will be to stick with whatever you do.

Morning Routine Customs

One of the most crucial habits that everyone should develop, according to many experts, is the morning ritual habit. This is due to studies that reveal an astounding 90% of prosperous people genuinely have morning ritual behavior. CEOs of major corporations, like Jack Dorsey of Twitter and IndraNooyi of PepsiCo, as well as powerful politicians like Margaret Thatcher, get up very early in the morning to do their rituals before leaving for work.

It's a terrific idea to get up early in the morning when it's peaceful to meditate, pray, or read motivational books and quotes. Turn off your electronics and concentrate on refreshing your thoughts at this unique moment. You are free to write in your journal, organize your entire day, and update it during this private time. You may prepare your body and mind for the upcoming day by doing this. Even better, you can decide which two of your daily duties are the most crucial and strive to complete them first thing in the morning to free up the afternoon for less important work.

Exercise is a crucial activity that you may fit into your morning routine. Running on a treadmill, even for only five to ten minutes, helps you decompress and increase your metabolism. It also clears your mind.

Last but not least, preparing meals for the entire day—all the way through dinner—is another habit of prosperous people's morning routines. Sure, you can occasionally eat out, but cooking at home is healthier and better, especially if you're watching your weight. Dining out is like a calorie-fest where the calories you would normally obtain from cooking your food are doubled, tripled, or even fivefold!

It would definitely be very tough for night owls to adjust to this lifestyle and change their behaviors at first. Try adjusting gradually. Every night, try to go to bed 15 minutes earlier so that you can wake up 15 minutes earlier. Continue this cycle until you become accustomed to going to bed and waking up early.

Experts in time management and behavior strongly advise establishing the morning ritual habit. Sure, it will be challenging, but that's why you should focus on forming one pattern at a time. Do this procedure gradually over several weeks? You should notice some results after about a month, at which point you'll be more productive and have a clearer idea of how to accomplish your objectives. Creating successful habits is crucial to your success.

The following activities can assist you in developing productive self-control routines:

First exercise: Make yourself start.

We are going to assist you in doing something you have been putting off for a while in this exercise. Locate a task you had intended to complete. It might be a book you've been meaning to read, a damaged item you've been meaning to mend around the house, or a project you've been meaning to tackle for your home. Currently, the likelihood is that you have made up a mental excuse for your inaction. You may be convincing yourself that you require additional data, time, funds, etc.

Consider this: "What's the first step I need to take to finish this?" Make yourself move in that direction. Whether you are ready or not doesn't matter; get going.

You'll come to understand that the hardest part of any endeavor is getting started but that as long as you don't give up and keep moving forwards, you can do it quickly.

Exercise 2: Make your bed wide.

You can finish making your bed in a matter of minutes. But a lot of us don't actually do it. How come? Since there is no justification for doing it and no repercussions if we don't. The devil is in the details, thus, spreading your bed is a disciplined act that can greatly assist you in leading a more ordered life.

Making your bed correctly should be your first priority when you get up next morning. You may even see a video online that demonstrates how to do it in a military-style manner. You will set yourself up for productivity in those two minutes after waking up, and you'll be surprised at how much more disciplined you will be for the remainder of the day.

Self-Control As The Primary Factor In Happiness

I enjoy discussing happiness all the time, but I never realized that having self-control could lead to happiness. I was astounded when I initially came across this knowledge, but I soon realized how valid the arguments were. I plotted various points in my life, and that's how it came out. Being disciplined makes me happy. Was it merely an accident? Let's solve it together.

"Yes, but are they happy?" was the title of a 2013 University of Chicago study carried out by Wilhelm Hoffman. The truth is that, for whatever reason, I frequently get the same response when I discuss self-discipline and make compelling arguments for restraint: "Yes, discipline is undoubtedly good, but are you happy if have to control yourself?" But it's okay to say that now.

You're happier when you can better manage yourself.

I have already stated in earlier issues that discipline is the primary predictor of success in life, as well as how long it will last. It also improves connections with people and your physical wellness. Happiness, however, is a whole other ballgame. Another 2017 study with over 5,000 individuals already demonstrates a clear connection between self-control and a feeling of subjective contentment. Where can one get such a strong, rigid addiction? This is, after all, entirely distinct from how we often conceptualize happiness, right? Sayings they make to us "Leave a life of freedom, partake in wine, dine out, sleep as much as you like, and do whatever brings you happiness and a long and enjoyable life." It turns out to be the exact opposite, in fact. "Go to sleep and wake up on time. Remember what you do and when you do it. You won't live a long and happy life unless you learn to control your impulses. This perspective undermines all we work towards while being swayed by public propaganda. Nevertheless, how can one account for such an effect?

The idea is that self-control involves more than just winning. There is always a reason behind a loss. Thus, discipline is more like a rivalry between competing objectives. Long-term success competes with short-term pleasure. People who are disciplined have learned to prioritize long-term goals over momentary pleasure. For instance, a disciplined person eats an apple and works out, as opposed to eating cake and lounging on the couch.

The irresponsible individual does the reverse. The ramifications for the future won't need to be explained. He'll be unwell, lethargic, and overweight. He will, of course, be unhappy. And the longer he lives in this manner, the more illnesses, inactivity, and excess weight he accumulates. He, therefore, hopes to quit it, cut down on his weight, and lead a healthy lifestyle one day. But it's difficult to break habits. Thus, discontent naturally arises. Though you can't, you want to get better. This is where misery stems from.

A disciplined person's mind is trained for long-term work, so they don't feel like eating cake. He is happier as a result. It is okay for him always to fight the want to consume the patty. He always takes the apple out of habit when he sees a cake next to it.

You only need to use discipline once to get used to the right behavior. Furthermore, you are free to stop when you have adapted to yourself. "A disciplined mind leads to happiness, a cheeky mind to suffering," the Dalai Lama once observed. He was correct. Being self-disciplined means being able to avoid temptation in the first place not giving in to it. In summary, disciplined individuals never deprive themselves of anything. All they want is something different. And they're delighted about this other thing. It is up to us to train our desires to be different.

A happy existence also involves having a high sense of self-worth. And despite the fact that it may come as a surprise, experts and academics believe that one of the primary components of great self-esteem is self-discipline. It transcends skill, looks, achievement, family dynamics, and other significant facets of our lives. For both adults and teenagers, the primary indicators of good self-esteem are self-control and discipline. And even in older people.

Why is this taking place? For self-respect is the foundation of self-esteem. And self-respect seems so easy. I respect myself when I perform to the standards I set for myself. For instance, if you don't achieve the success you expect from yourself, you'll feel low about yourself. However, if the expectation is reasonable, you'll feel more confident.

Thus, in addition to promoting achievement and prolonging life, self-discipline also enhances interpersonal connections, elevates our self-esteem, and makes us happy!

It Takes Self-Control to Achieve Success in Life

Success in any field of work is correlated with your ability to define yourself, manage yourself, control yourself, and mold yourself. According to Elbert Hubbard, "Self- disciplineistheabilityto make yourselfdowhatyou should do, when you should do it, whether you feellikeitor not." Individuals can form the following habits to shape their bright future: moral orientation, outcome orientation, action orientation, people orientation, health orientation, honesty, integrity, and self-discipline.

Make a clear decision regarding the new excellent habit. If you wish to improve your self-discipline, write out your goals on paper or stand in front of a mirror and declare, "I am an exceptionally well-defined individual in everything I do." This will boost your self-confidence. As often as possible and with as much enthusiasm and participation as you can, repeat this.

Think of yourself as though you already had the new healthy habit type. Imagine yourself already becoming exactly the person you want to be in the future. Remember that mental pictures activate and accentuate your intuition. Every change in your life and personality begins with a difference in your mental portrait. Regularly combine your imaginative thoughts with your positive affirmations.

Empathize with the confirmation and the impression. Please spend a few minutes every day to truly feel what it's like to be the admiring, exceptional, and beautiful human being that you have decided to become. Begin your new healthy habit with confidence. Assume the character and act as though you were hired to perform in the play or movie. The more you behave as though you have already formed the habit, the more you actually transform into the person you have always desired to be.

Inform others that you have decided to create this new habit. By telling others, you encourage and support yourself. However, don't share this with anyone who isn't a close friend. Additionally, you compel yourself to act consistently in line with your new goals since you are aware that others are watching. Review your development progress frequently and on a regular basis. Summarise your actions throughout the day in relation to the values and habits you are attempting to establish at the end of the day.

Self-Control And Sales

"Without a sale, nothing occurs."

Sales are a crucial factor in determining a company's success or failure. The biggest obstacle to a successful sales career is rejection fear. Many salespeople start engaging in "displacement" behaviors, like reducing the number of calls they make, browsing the internet, chatting with coworkers, moving documents, and so on, in an effort to prevent being turned down. Recall that a salesperson is only truly productive when they are speaking with prospects—people who can and will purchase a reasonable length of time—over the phone or in person.

It's critical to invest more time in sales with more qualified prospects. Make it a routine to visit or call on more potential customers. Increasing the number of connections with customers will enhance sales. The term for it is the Law of Probabilities.

There are two things you need to do to succeed in sales.

There will never be a shortage of possibilities. There should always be more potential customers to call than there is time in the day.

[6] Reading, studying, and listening to audio programs can all help you develop your skills in prospecting, presenting, and closing sales. Remember that you can learn any craft related to sales.

A successful salesperson has no fear of rejection since they are optimistic. They will be able to call prospects without losing enthusiasm as a result.

Cash And Self-Control

The main reason people fail financially is because they need to make more money. It's an inability to exercise restraint and an inclination to put off enjoying something right now. Most people have a propensity to spend all of their money right away. Our early years shaped our conditioned reaction to associate purchasing with enjoyment. When we were younger, we used to spend all of our money on candy. That was why we were happy. These days, having cash is equal to having pleasure. When you get money, your first thought is usually on what you can buy to get that temporary "high," happiness, or other fun.

Our objective is to rewire our financial reflexes so that saving money is associated with enjoyment. Start saving by opening a financial freedom account. Think on the big picture. Just learning how to save money can make you feel stronger and more in control of your life. According to common belief, "it takes money to make money." The larger the amount of money you have and the possibilities you have to use it wisely to increase the rate of return on those funds, The more money and options you have to manage those funds wisely. Hence, they give an even higher rate of return as your financial freedom account grows.

Financial gurus advise saving between 15 and 20 percent of your income in order to become financially independent in the future. You can gradually accomplish this by using the one percent technique, which suggests that you begin setting aside 1% of your income and learn to survive on the remaining 99 percent. Every month, you increase your savings rate by 1%. Consequently, you will have saved about 10% of your salary by year's end.

Setting Goals

Setting objectives is something that everyone understands, but most individuals only come to appreciate its significance after moving on in life. Establishing goals can help you stay focused on what matters, offer you control and a feeling of direction, motivate you, and make you feel good. But more than merely establishing goals won't cut it; the secret to unlocking these gifts is to set them correctly.

Ways to Make Goals

Let's start by discussing goal-setting mistakes. If you have been interested in personal development for some time, you may be familiar with goal-setting in general or with modern goal-setting. This method of goal-setting has the drawback of not enabling you to identify your true desires and desires at their core. Consider the following scenario: you decide that you want a raise, so you go after it and have a chance of succeeding. This goal's drawback is that it offers no personal explanation, which could lead you to pursue an entirely unrelated course from your own desires. Any objective can be broken down by asking "Why?" as a follow-up question. Again, using that scenario, you desire a raise. Why now? To get a new car, you might advise. The conversation can continue like this: "I want a raise so that I can afford a new car because I keep comparing myself to my neighbors and I saw that they have a better car than mine." Therefore, raising your salary isn't the answer, and that's how most people fall victim to goal-setting and end up lost in the process.

There is another approach to goal-setting that avoids the same pitfalls. Before you set any goals, it's important to understand your "Why." Since most of the time our objectives are linked to entirely different outcomes, if you keep asking yourself these kinds of questions, you'll eventually find your roots and, occasionally, acquiring a new car won't be such a bad idea after all. Not only can answer your own questions and organising your "Why" help you avoid meaningless goals, but they will also serve as a source of motivation. With these considerations in mind, this is how I go about making goals:

● To begin with, you must ensure that you have a strong desire to accomplish a goal, that you have faith in your ability to succeed, and that you anticipate success. The only thing limiting you will be your faith.

● Set priorities in your life: determine what matters most to you at this time in terms of your work, finances, health, etc.

● After identifying your "Why," make a list of your two to three year long goals and put it in front of various aspects of your life.

| Write down the steps you need to take this year to accomplish your long-term objectives. For weeks, months, or a year, short-term goals could be set.

You will have your goals on paper once you have put out your short-term objectives. Remember to apply "Why" as a filter intentionally. Here are a few pointers:

🎯 Really, you need to put down your goals and follow your instincts to determine how you're going to get there.

🎯 Consider large. Never set limits for yourself; realistic goals are the best kind, especially for long-term objectives.
❏

Avoid attempting to know everything with certainty. There are many unknowns in life, and you can never predict what will occur in the future. Who can say? It may turn out differently than you could have ever dreamed.

❦ Establish attainable targets for the short-term objectives.

Establishing objectives will also support your self-esteem growth. A sense of success from achieving your goals will boost your self-esteem. Your short-term objectives should be something that you can readily accomplish when you are just starting out. Avoid getting too attached to them right away. As your self-worth increases in the future, you can scale this up.

Develop An Ability To Focus

The capacity to concentrate lies inside you. To improve your ability to concentrate, you should put your body, mind, and emotions on your side.

Your mind is diverted by daydreaming or focusing on too many things at once. When the body's basic needs aren't met or it is fatigued, it can become disturbed. Because you lack a heart or because you are dealing with an emotional issue that is taking up your time, you are able to deflect your feelings.

It assists you in determining your goals, setting deadlines, removing distractions, and concentrating on your objectives within this time frame. Making your workstation comfortable and anticipating your body's needs—such as hunger, thirst, or fatigue—will assist.

Decide who your objective is.

Decide exactly what you want to focus on and why. The most important step is this one. That's where you decide to concentrate. Now is the time to ask yourself, "What do I want to do?" It helps you visualize what you want to accomplish. This picture serves as a reminder to focus. It's important to specify "what" and "what" you hope to achieve. Make it easy. Make it easy. Make it plain. Make it plain. To ensure clarity and simplicity, try stating your goal in just one line and visualizing the most basic achievement you can imagine.

To visualize something straightforward to concentrate on: Tell me your one-liner objective: "I want to finish this book," "I want to get in the best shape of my life," "I want to finish my introduction," etc. Consider it a straightforward image. You are going to take a picture of this to serve as a reminder of your focus.

Imagine your appearance if the desired outcomes are achieved. Are you feeling terrific, or just good?

Decide why you would like this to occur. Keep it striking yet simple enough. It can be for someone else or you.

Link it to your principles. Linking your actions to your values is one method to focus your attention. For instance, you might value fun, growth, learning, or greatness. If you love fun, turn it into a game. If you enjoy reading, try to squeeze in some new education while you're on the road. If you value excellence, figure out how to make your approach better.

You can recall your focus just by outlining your objective. You can use a basic picture to work your way back from the target. You can be inspired to take action by this image. It can also serve as a guide for you as you proceed, and this image provides a simple means of refocusing once you have moved out of the way.

Note: Concentrating on something greater than yourself for the better can help you inspire yourself and help you focus more on yourself. This is particularly strong if you respect contribution or aid to raise or restore others.

Could you write it down? Enter your target, and the steps to get there are an easy way to focus. It is a short reminder and helps to free your mind to concentrate better. Use simple lists and bullets to chart and recall your path. You can use lists to write stuff to help you concentrate on a simple task and schedule your day, week, month, or year.

To improve your focus by using writing, write down your goals. List them as points of a single bullet. With a simple list, you will know what you want to achieve.

Specify specific steps or activities for your goals. This will make it easy for you to still know your next step or assignment without working too hard to recall what will follow. It allows you to keep focused, especially when you're distracted or frustrated.

This is just another falsehood since corporations don't genuinely want to change the world. This is different from the reason they invest. Their goal is to maximize their financial gains.

Did you know that many companies frame their goal and vision statements with grand ideals? They wish to treat their supervisors with courtesy and kindness. Employers who pay less can get employees to dedicate more time and effort.

This litany of lies may go on forever. There are many corporate lies, and staff members are well aware of them. The best course of action when you hear a lie is to remain alert and put your own interests ahead of the lie. Reject an offer that you believe compromises your moral character or jeopardizes your health. Refuse to believe lies.

Willpower and Self-Determination in Your Online Life Brightness

Many things need to be put into place in your online business before you can succeed, but few things are as important as self-control and willpower. You will be challenged in so many ways when building your business that these two qualities will become indispensable to you in nearly every aspect of your life. There's no good excuse for putting off or not acting upon many things that we all know are vitally important for your online business.

Frequently, you may want to take on tasks that you know would be beneficial and crucial for your online business, but if you don't really take action to complete them, you'll notice that time becomes scarce and very little gets accomplished. This kind of situation happens to most of us, particularly when we lack self-discipline and have poor willpower. So, continue reading because I'll go over a few strategies for developing self-control and self-discipline.

It would be best if you didn't continue believing that you are self-sufficient and disciplined. Rather, I will demonstrate how to acquire these attributes to impact your life significantly. You will be on your way to realizing that you are becoming more self-disciplined and determined when you begin eliminating the bad habits that prevent you from moving forward, such as sloth, overindulgence in food, smoking, and ritualization. It is really necessary to possess more of these attributes in order to succeed in your online business.

How, then, do you acquire willpower? What is your initial understanding of willpower? You are erroneous if you believe, as many do, that weightlifting is a very tough or challenging exercise, or that you must tense your body and breathe in order to perform it. I was hoping you wouldn't believe that because I'm going to demonstrate several strategies that will persuade you that developing a willow tree is not difficult.

When you disregard unimportant, unnecessary, and unhealthy thoughts, emotions, behaviors, and responses that don't elevate you, you are demonstrating your worthlessness. You own this energy, which you can access whenever you need it to achieve your goals.

We'll go over some later exercises you can perform to gain a lot of willpower. Let's now discuss self-discipline and its importance for both your life and your business. You may argue that when you make decisions for your business and see them through to completion, you experience some self-doubt since you are not granted quick gratification and freedom to stray from your intended course of action. That's actually a good definition of self-discipline because your actions enabled you to stick to the path you had previously chosen.

Is this something that every person needs in their life? Of course! However, as we've already stated, you wouldn't stick to your decisions and would struggle to achieve your business goals. When you have it, your actions, ideas, and behavior are in line with living a better and more fulfilling life since your inner strength and willpower will enable you to overcome negative traits like procrastination, laziness, and lack of focus. This will allow you to pursue any goal you have in mind for your online business.

Therefore, why wouldn't you learn self-discipline? You already know how important and necessary it is for success in both your personal and professional lives; thus, embrace and further develop it. Keep in mind that lacking discipline could cause you to fail in achieving your goals. On the other hand, the behaviors listed above that show you have a self-disciplined nature also lead to self-assurance, inner strength, and self-regard, as well as total happiness and contentment.

In business, there are many obstacles and challenges to overcome on the way to success, achievement, and prosperity. Your goal is to overcome them all in order to succeed in whatever you do. To overcome other negative behaviors such as drug addiction, drinking, eating disordered foods, and other unhealthy habits like smoking, drinking, and sleeping, you must possess patience, persistence, and inner strength.

In addition to the attributes listed above, the following is what self-discipline may accomplish for you:

It enables you to control and manage your anger, impulsivity, hunger, and several other natural reactions.

You can avoid numerous types of unnecessary temptations, such as excessive eating, gambling, gambling, or watching too much television.

It can prevent you from giving up when things get difficult in your personal or professional life by giving you the willpower to carry on.

With it, you can build wonderful relationships with other people by not being easily offended or disturbed by things that other people occasionally say or do to you.

It gives you greater control over the urge to achieve the goals you set for yourself in your internet business, as well as complete control over your responses, needs, and thoughts.

There are numerous benefits that self-discipline can offer, but how can you cultivate the inner traits of self-control and self-discipline? Well, the ability to gain willpower varies greatly and is largely dependent on your desire to do so.

It also doesn't require a significant amount of work to do. Don't trust people who tell you that the only way to become well-off is to endure severe suffering or physical mutilation.

Actually, anyone can become powerful with willpower alone—all it takes is the challenge of eliminating what you know to be unhealthy for you in numerous aspects of your personal and professional life. You become stronger based on how many of these negative habits you are able to break by putting up negative and pointless things that consume your time and make you feel weak. Putting this process into practice is the necessary challenge to make your life more engaging, fascinating, and fascinating.

The well-wisher you have is not something that can be fulfilled in a single day. You can only develop it gradually over time, and it's something that doesn't depend on emotions, sentiments, lack of focus enthusiasm, or even optionism. Rather, this increased ability, which develops over time and, if it becomes a habit, is something that is so unique that you can use it repeatedly whenever and wherever you need it.

Increasing Control Over Oneself

It's not simple to resist easy things in favour of hard things, or to say no to all of your inclinations. It is consuming an apple rather than a hamburger. It is about not snoozing the alarm for the fifth time, but rather rising at the first sound of the alarm. Instead of surfing through social media, it involves all those anxiety-inducing duties that lead you towards your dreams. Self-control goes by many names, such as restraint, discipline, and willpower. Whatever you name it, it usually contributes significantly to your well-being and achievement. Determining whether you should spend or save, exercise or remain home, lose or maintain your temper, or succumb to the dark side of procrastination may all be accomplished with the aid of self-control. Ineffective impulse control is also considered a sign of a number of diseases, including OCD, depression, and ADHD. It also includes impulse control problems, including obsessive shoplifting, skin picking, and hair pulling.

It could be very subtle at times. You may accomplish all that needs to be done, just not just now. This is known as productive procrastination. Cleaning the toilet is a good deed, but not if it keeps you from doing other tasks. Thus, apply the following techniques to enhance your self-control the next time you are tempted to have a burger.

Prioritising the Hardest Tasks

Your degree of self-control also tends to wane as the day goes on. In a Harvard study, participants were asked to identify whether there were more dots on the left or right side of the screen after a brief display of a pattern consisting of twenty drops. After making their choice and receiving some money, the participants endured one more dot flash, totaling roughly one hundred flashes. But there was a catch. If the participants consistently selected the correct side of the screen, regardless of whether the response was right or not, they would receive ten times more money. Therefore, even in cases where the answer was incorrect, there was strong motivation to select the correct side. Remarkably, compared to everyone who was tested in the afternoon, everyone who chose to participate in the experiment in the morning, between 8 am and noon, was less likely to submit a few more right-handed responses.

Researchers know this as the "morning morality effect." Good individuals struggle to resist doing bad things, like lying to get more money, because their energy levels fluctuate throughout the day. It does not, however, serve as a justification for any form of negative behavior; rather, it educates people that they should not count on ultimate resistance to temptation. Therefore, it is advised that you begin your day by tackling the most difficult duties. It can strengthen your self-control and keep you from giving in to temptation.

Adapting the surroundings to Modify the Conduct

When the day is over, what should a morning bird do? What should a night owl do in the early hours of the morning? Throwing temptation to the wind is one of the best strategies for overcoming it. Just don't buy Skittles if you can't resist eating them at midnight. Try everything to keep yourself off social media if you find yourself browsing through it while at work. To put it plainly, never put yourself in a position to fail. Just as you wouldn't let a youngster loose in a video game store, don't expect to be able to resist temptation when you're anxious, worn out, or hungry. You can take action by clearing the area of temptation. If your environment can function as self-control, then you don't need to.

Monitoring Your Progress

The ability to alter the phenomenon being witnessed is inherent in observation. The same applies to keeping tabs on your credit card balance. To keep track of anything that is likely to undermine your self-control, you will need to keep a log or a tracker. You can track anything by keeping a diet journal, an exercise journal, or a sleep log. Monitoring is the process of keeping a record of everything you do. If you are not attentive, things will get out of hand. Therefore, it will benefit you more if you focus and keep track of your development. Additionally, monitoring is an excellent treatment for impulse control problems like skin picking and hair pulling. As you observe, you can alter what you are seeing, which will undoubtedly affect your behavior.

Observing Yourself at Work

If you're stuck at your desk and want to maintain healthy habits, you can put a mirror right next to you. It operates according to the same monitoring principle. You'll be less likely to do things like watch yourself scarf down a meal or browse social media when you have work to accomplish. A fantastic substitute is to choose to work in public. If all you do when working from home is browse social media, you can use a shared office or a coffee shop.

Accepting Your Diversions, But Not Right Now

"I will do this later" is the most popular motto shared by all procrastinators. Why not attempt to switch the order of what you want to do now and what you want to do later? Tell yourself that you will attend to the distractions later rather than completing your work later. Tell yourself that you will check social media once you've completed the current work if you notice yourself drifting off course from an important one and focusing on something else distracting. That is true—it is simpler said than done. However, if you continue to practice this idea, you will gradually be able to build up more self-control.

Observing the Large Image

Research indicates that the development of self-control can be aided by abstract or higher-level thinking. Put, when people are able to see past specific details and are drawn to the bigger picture, they are more likely to practice self-control. For example, the incremental steps required to obtain the end result can easily lead to frustration when working on a large project. To help promote self-control, consider reminding yourself and your team of the ultimate goal instead of giving up. By keeping discouragement at bay, it is accomplished.

Understanding the Consequences of Sleep Deficit

According to a Washington University study, sleep deprivation can quickly deplete glucose in the prefrontal brain. As a result, it causes the fuel needed for self-control to run out. Sleep aids in its restoration in this regard. The following day, it was discovered to have an impact on whether or not an action was morally righteous, such as forging fake invoices. Comparing those who slept for longer than the first group, all of those who slept for roughly six hours or less were more likely to engage in deviant job behaviours. There's a claim that companies need to treat sleep with greater dignity. Executives and managers must always keep in mind that the more they encourage their staff to work long hours, arrive at work early, and take constant calls, the more unethical behaviour they will encourage. You'll notice that your capacity for self-control has increased to new heights if you get adequate sleep.

Engaging in Exercise

Do you find it challenging to choose an exercise program due to your time constraints? For you, there is excellent news. You only need to engage in a brief, modest exercise routine to build your self-control muscles. It has been discovered that even a little exercise helps to improve the blood and oxygen flow to this region. In return, it can readily improve your capacity for self-control. No matter how busy you are, it makes no difference. To raise your degree of self-control, try including quick workouts into your schedule.

Overcoming Failure With Self-Control

You'll discover that you can start altering your thinking after self-discipline is practiced. Because you don't believe that you actually need other people to validate or succeed in life, you won't be terrified of how you appear to them. It is sufficient for you to draw from your wellspring of self-acceptance and self-love.

You see, what paralyzes you is the dread of failing. To break free from its hold, you must be able to defeat that beast, that impediment in your way. You will accept that you failed because of your self-discipline, which will serve as both your sword and shield in this situation. Pause and make an effort to name one individual in your life who has never experienced failure. It would be difficult to locate someone who has never failed in life. Even helpless newborns have failed at something; maybe they coughed because they were unable to complete the suck-swallow-breathe cycle, which prevents them from choking or suffocating when nursing. It happens to everyone, no matter how large or small.

Try to recall how many mistakes you have made in your life at this point. Can you estimate the number? Most likely not—it isn't easy to count them. You may have failed at something even today. It is possible that you were unable to write the correct letter the first time and had to use the delete key on your phone or keyboard to remove the incorrect letter. You may have stumbled. Perhaps you misplaced something. Nevertheless, it's likely that in the recent 24 hours, you have failed at something.

Was everything lost because of the typo? In no way. Did you have a really bad day because you dropped the cookie you wanted to eat? Most likely not. It is not necessary for failure to be the huge deal that a lot of people portray it to be.

You have to learn to conquer your fear of failing when you're prepared to face down and conquer failure completely.

To achieve this, you should develop your self-discipline. Perseverance is a trait that comes with self-control. You won't be afraid of failing and will keep trying to be successful even when you do. It will instruct you on how to strengthen your will. Despite your fear of failing, you will embrace whatever is going on and take on the issue head-on rather than fighting to get yourself started. You'll overcome your doubts and anxieties so that you may attempt. That in itself enables you to change your perspective from one in which failure is interpreted as the end of the world to one in which you see failure as the catalyst for something greater. Failure can teach you something. Failure can make you stronger. Mistakes shape one's character. Failing is just another way of saying don't do something. Because failure is genuinely good for you, the variety of proverbs and clichés about how it can be better for you than unqualified success is almost endless.

It's time for you to go over three distinct approaches that will assist you in gaining the self-control required to learn how to overcome failure. Try to come up with situations in which you could use these techniques in your own life as you go through them. It is a nice surprise to learn that these are effective and that you can actually address and get rid of your fear of failing.

Conclusion

You've been on a quest to develop strong self-discipline thanks to this book. You and others will soon start to notice the results if you implement the advice with zeal and regularity in your life. You'll learn to approach life, goal-setting, and achievement in general with greater positivity. Aspirations and goals that you once thought were too difficult will become doable, if not easy.

Keep in mind that you only get one chance to live the life you want to live, as far as anyone can tell. You are too busy to continue squandering time being unreliable, unmotivated, and lethargic. Let this book serve as a reminder that in the end, only you have the ability to design the life you want, if nothing else. Instead of becoming debilitating, let this realisation be uplifting. You'll be astounded at what you can do if you set high standards for yourself and fight to change your perspective.

Please think about writing a review if this book has been beneficial to you so that others can start the process of transforming their life and kicking their own asses!

Get out there and begin changing the world for the better!

www.ingramcontent.com/pod-product-compliance
Lightning Source LLC
Chambersburg PA
CBHW052151110526
44591CB00012B/1933